MW01138291

Serious Revenge

And the Art of Stealth Payback

By Tarrin P. Lupo

Cover Art by Ruby Nicole Hilliard

Edited by Starr O'Hara

The cover is a picture of my neighbor who was seeking justice for a stolen bike. Her expensive bike was stolen from her back yard and the thief left his bike behind. She took the thief's bike and got payback by chaining to this tree and letting the world know.

Porcupine Publications

Porcupine Publications

ISBN 978-1-937311-14-8

Printed with the spirit of

This book is for all of us who have gotten screwed out there and have thought there was nothing we could do about it.

Table of Contents

Introduction i

CHAPTER ONE: 1
BECOME INVISIBLE

CHAPTER TWO: 9
INFORMATION LETS YOUOWN YOUR VICTIM

CHAPTER THREE: 21
THE LEGAL ROUTE

CHAPTER FOUR 31
VERY NASTY REVENGE IDEAS

A WORD OF CAUTION 63

Introduction

I only recommend these ideas for entertainment and humorous purposes. Keeping that in mind, let's begin.

So you're looking for really mean revenge ideas? Is the stuff on the web just not meaningful enough for you? Most of the stuff out there that's free consists of fun pranks, gags, or practical jokes. No one really teaches you how to destroy some jerk's life. If you want serious, hardcore revenge, you are in the right place. The contents of this e-book will teach you how to ruin somebody's life, so only use it in self-defense.

Do not take this information lightly and use it only on victims who have drastically wronged you.

The information in this book is like a gun. It can be used for good or evil depending on who wields it. If you want to use this information to hurt innocent people I hope these ideas blow up in your face and Karma kicks you right in the ass. If you are seeking justice and nobody will help you, then this book is for you.

I strive to live my life by the ideas liberty and the non-aggression principle. That basically means I don't believe in initiating force toward others to accomplish any goal. I ONLY believe in the use of force after somebody has deprived me of freedom, livelihood, or property. I am one of the most peaceful and forgiving people on the planet. I would never strike first and would not knowingly do somebody wrong or destroy someone's property or livelihood. With all that being said, unfortunately, some predators in the world see someone who lives by the non-aggression principle as an easy target. It is an invitation to them to try to cheat and take advantage of you. In my early life I felt like I was becoming a doormat, always getting used and scammed. Where I went wrong was I expected people to be honest, good, and actually keep their word to me. Most people were honest and good, but I had many run-ins with opportunists and predatory jerks.

I got sick of being screwed over and never getting justice. Many scam artists screw people over and smile about it. The con man knows the system is useless to try and use against them. If you ever tried to get justice with the system you know it is laughable. Even if by a miracle you win a judgment it is almost impossible to collect retribution. Soon one realizes they need to make their own justice and forget about using the legal route.

I am sure you know those kinds of conmen. They can be easy to like or even to fall in love with. You want to help them and believe they are good. Unfortunately, they take and take and take. They betray your kindness and backstab you. They have no conscience about defrauding you and moving on to do it to their next victim like a locust. Do you know this person? I'll bet you do!

In my own life, I would try to seek justice through the legal realm with absolutely no help whatsoever. The government is corrupt and completely worthless. It just makes you spend more money you don't have and protects the person who victimized you. When I used the system I realized I was getting victimized twice. I also came to the realization that I would have to take things into my own hands to get justice. I feel the best way to get justice is to get revenge.

A good rule of thumb is to only cause as much pain as was caused you. You need to keep payback balanced. If you deal out way more payback then they deserve, the universe has a funny way of making sure you stay in balance and it will come back and bite you in the butt.

Okay, so let us get down to the nuts and bolts. First thing is first. You need to learn how to become anonymous.

CHAPTER ONE:

BECOME INVISIBLE

I will teach you how to attack somebody without them knowing who you are. I am a big believer of stealth revenge. It keeps you out of legal trouble and protects your assets.

First, let's discuss human nature for a moment. It is human nature to always see yourself as a victim. The victim role is a nice place to be. Everyone feels sorry for you and it allows your logical mind to justify doing wrong to other people. Let me explain that better.

I have seen this so many times from patients, roommates, girlfriends and business colleagues. A person will cheat you and then portray themselves as the victim. I was a doctor and patients would sing my praises during their round of treatments. Afterwards, they would not pay me when their insurance didn't cover all the treatments and they would disappear. When I would try to collect what they owed me I would find out their tune had dramatically changed. I'd learn they had trashed me around town, saying what an awful doctor I was, that I had ripped them off.

In order to justify not paying me, and basically stealing from me, they had to vilify me in their mind. I guarantee the person who victimized you has probably vilified you so they can justify screwing you over in their own minds.

What's this got to do with becoming invisible and attacking by stealth, you ask? It is a warning about human nature. If you openly strike back, you are begging for retaliation. The retaliation will be on a much nastier level of attack then the original insult.

As tempting as it is to rub your revenge in the face of your victim, it creates a revenge war mentality. Some people ALWAYS have to have the last word and they will keep attacking you until it escalates completely out of control. This is how people get shot or run over.

Yes, I know this is a very passive aggressive mentality, but trust me; you want to attack anonymously and be able to deny it. It will drive your victim crazy. They will suspect it is you, but be unable to prove it, and that in itself creates its own joy.

Let's get down to brass tacks. In order to become invisible, you will have to spend some money. Unfortunately, there is no way around spending a little money because you need what I call "revenge tools." I will recommend as many free things as I can, but with some products, you do not want to take chances and compromise.

Many of the serious revenge ideas require you to use a computer. First, you need to hide your IP address. For you who are not computer savvy, let me explain.

IP ADDRESSES

You might not be aware of it but your computer has a number address that it leaves on everything you look at on the net. It is like leaving a card with your home address on it everywhere you go in the electronic world. Scary, isn't it!

Tech savvy people can trace anything you do back to your IP address and find you. You will need to hide your IP address first before you start your attacks. The best way to do this is to use a program that will obscure your IP address. These days there are tons of good programs out there that let you hide or spoof your IP. Just search for "IP Address spoof" or "Hide IP" and you can find a good one.

You can also combine these programs with www.anonymization.com, which is a search tool bar that you can install to add multiple privacy levels. The more cloaks of privacy there are, the better. There is even a service called www.startpage.com that allows you to surf completely anonymously. It is sort of like Google without all the spyware and tracking of your information.

It is rumored that if someone is good enough to bust through all your walls of defense, they can track you by your computer's serial number and software registration. If you are really doing some hardcore payback, I suggest you use an anonymous phone and cash. Also buy a random, used computer to use in your revenge strikes. If it is traced, the name won't be yours!

CASH CARDS

Always use cash if you can. Anytime you order with a credit card, check, or anything with your name attached, you can be easily be tracked. You can always use money orders, but some places will not take them and they have a habit of disappearing when you mail them in. You will need to hide your money trail, which means cash or gift cards in an alias name.

Did you ever wonder how immigrants are able to get credit cards without a social security number or ID? When you inspect closer, you'll find they are not credit cards, but are debit cash cards or gift cards. These cards work wherever credit cards work. You can buy anonymous gift credit cards or debit cards everywhere for a nominal fee.

The easiest place to get one without revealing your identity is a check cashing business. If they require a name, go ahead and use your victim's name and address, and say that you don't have a picture ID. The check cashing places usually could care less who you are and will give you a card as long as you've got cash with which to pay their fees. These days, gas stations and drug stores are great locations to obtain a debit cash card, too.

Keep your eyes open, because many people just throw these cards out when they are empty and get another. If you find an empty one, you can refill it and your identity will remain safe.

UNTRACEABLE PHONE

You also need to hide your phone number. Some of these revenge ideas require you to make anonymous calls. Find a coin operated public phone, if you can, but even that can be traced back to you if there are security cameras in the area.

Another good way to remain anonymous is to use a VOIP phone. For you non computer savvy folks, that is a phone the works using the Internet. It is much cheaper then a real phone, but you need high speed internet in order to use it. The best bang for the buck hands down is Skype or Magic Jack. Skype has been around a while, but it is a neat system that works wonderfully for what you need. You can buy just the outgoing phone line so you will not have a phone number that someone can call you back on.

When the victim receives a phone call, the phone number will appear on their caller ID like this: 00001123456. This is a great way to hide yourself.

When using Skype, remember to hide your IP address and pay with an anonymous gift card.

There are also many programs where you can change what your caller ID says. You can change it to Planned Parenthood, or Investigation and Fraud Department. With a little imagination you can have tons of fun with this technology. Just search for "caller ID spoofer".

You can also buy a prepaid cell phone with an alias and call people anonymously, but they get expensive quickly! Just use the *67 command to block your caller ID and this phone will be damn near impossible to trace. If you are doing hardcore paybacks you will want to try to buy an older model without a GPS tracker built in. You can still find these on Ebay if you look hard enough. If you are lucky enough to find one, it will be impossible to track you down through your phone.

WEBSITES and EMAIL

Some of these payback ideas require you to use anonymous emails or set up bogus websites. If you're tech savvy, this is a no brainer and available everywhere. If you are not tech savvy, I can help. You can set up an anonymous email at Gmail, Yahoo or Thunderbird. You can set up a free anonymous website if you just search the net for a minute. As long as you have protected your IP well you will be good to go.

Want to really cover your butt and make yourself impossible to track? Do all three of these things in order:

1. Hide your IP address;
2. Create a free email with a fake name;
3. Use a third party mail out service like www.hushmail.com . What this allows is a hard-to-track go between for your victim's email and yours.

PROTECT YOURSELF

Don't be a target yourself so somebody else can use these ideas on you. The next thing you want to tackle is your network. I am not trying to be overly technical, but I do need to explain some basics in case you don't know.

Many computers are on wireless networks. The computer sends information through the air into a network wireless modem. If you're not sure if you have one, it will be a big blinking box with an antenna connected to a phone line or cable.

A wireless network makes it so easy to steal your information, hack your computer, and basically screw with you. They are an open invitation for mischief.

Make sure you at least have your network password protected. It is pretty easy to do and you can find the option under your network button in your control panel. That won't stop the experts, but it will deter most people. Also, turn off your wireless when you're not using it. I mean literally unplug the thing from the wall. I know it can be a pain, but it cuts the avenue for hackers when it is not in use.

Shred Everything! If you really make someone mad, or if you have a stalker, you need to do this. Your stalker will take your trash and clone your identity to keep an eye out on all your business.

Also, shred computer files using a shredder program. It is surprisingly easy to recover anything you have deleted unless you electronically shred it. There are lots of free programs out there if you search "data wiping" or "data shredding".

Of course, turn on your firewalls and set passwords, but you also want to eliminate and protect your computer from spy ware. Run spyware checks constantly. Spy software is getting so sneaky these days.

Try to use a land line or computer phone line whenever possible. It is surprisingly easy to clone a cell phone and listen in to all your calls.

Please remember, you really have NO privacy rights at all when it comes to the government. They can break through any firewall you throw up without a warrant. Any email you send can be read and used against you. Thank you, Patriot Act, for taking a big dump on our privacy rights! Some of these ideas involve using the government on your victim. The only way to protect yourself is to become completely anonymous so that even if they can see the emails, they have no idea who sent it.

CHAPTER TWO:

INFORMATION LETS YOU OWN YOUR VICTIM

How can you become a detective and gather information about your victim?

You might be dealing with an ex you were intimate with and/or married to, a backstabbing friend, bad business partner or stalker, but one thing remains the same. Information is king! It is amazing to see somebody who was destroying your life suddenly back off in fear. It feels great to turn the tables on your victim and have the ability to destroy their life the way they tried to destroy yours.

Let me share a story out of my own life to prove this point.

I had a guy I knew at my first job who was jealous of me. He was constantly doing things to draw attention to me and my then devious ways. He was a busy body who would not mind his own business. Needless to say it got very old, and I got in trouble every time I came in late and left early.

I decided to turn the tables and become my own busy body.

I started spying on him; I listened to his calls while hiding around the corner. I knew he had a girlfriend who always came in and ate at the restaurant we were working in. Right after she left, he would always take a break and get on the phone.

One day I overheard him say to someone that his girlfriend was leaving town and that he could stay over for the night but would need a ride to work.

The next day before his shift I hid in a bush outside the restaurant with a camera and waited for him to get dropped off. A car pulled up and he got out. He walked over to the driver, learned in and delivered a kiss. SNAP! I took a picture. You can imagine my surprise when I realized the person he was kissing was a man.

Later, when I was alone with him, I told him that I saw him get dropped off. He got very quiet and I let him know I didn't appreciate him constantly getting me in trouble at work.

He got the message and never talked about me again at work. Had it gone further, and he did not comply with my wishes, I had plenty of ammo to use against him. I had a picture of him kissing a man, license plate # of the boyfriend, and I knew his girlfriend.

The right information on someone can let you own them. It is an ironic time we live in when the only way to get someone to act ethically is to force them into it by being unethical.

The way to get someone to back off or to leave you alone is to hold information over their head.

LOW TECH SPYING

There are, of course, so many ways to do this. You can use some low tech spying by just hiding out of sight and listening to your victim's conversations! You would be amazed at the dirt you can dig up on a co-worker or ex by just hiding right out of sight and listening.

Start off by simply spying on your victim. Cell phones are unbelievable these days and you can film and record easily without being obvious. See if you can catch them in compromising positions. You can even go super old school and swear a simple disguise like a hat and big sunglass. Stay far away from them to take your photos or simply plant your phone and leave it recording where you know they hang out. It is amazing the things your phone will pick up in a break room.

You can also steal their mail out of their box, but I advise against this strategy. Although this is highly illegal and you can go to jail if caught, the amount of information you can get from a mailbox is amazing. The safer and legal way to do it is just wait for them to throw out their mail and dig it out of the trash.

To open a letter without tearing it up use this very old technique that still works well. Use just a little water and wet the flap on the back especially where the glue seal is. Stick it in the microwave at low or medium heat and watch for the steam to buckle the glue. When you see this pull it out and open it quickly. When you're done reading the mail, just apply a little glue to the flap, push down and seal it back up

If you don't give a damn about breaking the law, then it is far better to reroute their mail to you at a fake address. It might be months before they figure it out. It is better to anonymously get a mail box and send their mail to an abandoned address or an old mailbox that nobody uses anymore. Just pick up a change of address form at the Post Office, fill it out, and drop it in a mail box.

If you really want to make this convincing, open the important mail you want to see using the microwave steam method. Then seal them back up and return the mail to the victim's mailbox. Copy the information you want, but don't forget to wear gloves when you do this. Then be careful when you return it to their box and remember to remove all the forwarding stickers. They will think they are still getting mail and you will get all their important information you want. When you get all the info you need, change their mail address back to normal and the victim will have never known.

The best way to gather information is also a safer legal way. Just take their trash bags. A ton of people still don't shred their papers and it is perfectly legal to just grab their trash bags on the road. You can find out all sorts of interesting things about your victim like:

All their utilities account numbers!

Their phone records and what numbers they call and when!

Their financial information, stocks, bonds, real estate and bank accounts!

Personal letters and cards!

Credit card and debit card information!

Receipts of where they go and what they buy!

Trash can be a goldmine of information to ruin somebody. This art is lovingly known as "dumpster diving."

You can also pay a little bit of money and buy a ton of information about somebody. Again you will want to pay for this anonymously. They have what are known as information farms all over the Internet. You can get your victims social security #, bank info, real estate transactions, etc. These information farms could care less what you do with the information, and it is truly amazing what they can find out on somebody for just $50.

HIGH TECH AND COMPUTER ATTACKS

I will try to keep this low tech for you non-computer savvy people and you can do more research about any ideas you like. My main goal is to make you aware of this technology and how to use it as weapons for revenge.

PHONES

Let us start with a phone attack. Being able to listen to people's phone conversations can allow you to create massive havoc in your victim's life. There are a few good ways to do this.

The first is the old fashioned phone jacking. If your victim has an old fashioned landline, you can find the outside phone jack and just plug in. The phone company has a little box on the outside of the house that has a jack with a short phone cable sticking into it. You can just plug a splitter into the jack outlet and run your own line. If you don't plan on spying this way too much, you can just buy a very long phone line and plug into the jack, as I just explained. Unfortunately, the long phone cable can be seen running from the house so you might want to do this at night and definitely remove the cable when you are done. Just park around the corner and listen in.

One can also buy a little device you can plug in that converts and sends the signal wirelessly to you. It is pretty pricey, but a less obvious form of phone jacking.

Do you want to get the victims phone records?

If you have the victim's cell phone number, account number and SS number you can usually get their phone records. Go to the homepage of the cell provider and type in their phone number. Ninety-nine per cent of the time, the victim has never bothered to set up an account online.

The cell provider might ask the last four digits of the SS number but that's about it. Just set up a new account and password, and have it emailed to your anonymous email address.

The provider will send you an email saying your account is set up and all you have to do is log back in. You will be able to search and print all their phone records online. You can also cause havoc by massively upgrading their plan to the most expensive choice, or cancelling their plan so they get slammed with fines.

If they happen to have set up their account online, you will need to call in and have the victim's information ready. Have their SS number, mother's maiden name and maybe their pet's name. Tell them to set up a new password because you forgot it and you have a new email address (your anonymous one). Make sure to cover yourself with a voice changer or disguise your voice, and also use an anonymous phone when calling in.

Cell phones are a different story. If their cell phone has a bluetooth wireless function, these can be jacked into pretty easily. This will only work in about a 30 foot radius, so this is only good for co-workers who sit close to you.

A better idea is to Blue Snarf a phone. What this means is you get your laptop within about 30 feet of a persons phone and you can hack into it and download all of their information. You can get their address book, phone numbers and calendar.

Just search "Bluetooth jacking" and "Snarfing".

A better way to attack a cell phone is to clone it. Cloning basically lets you reprogram your phone so that it is a duplicate of your victim's. Whenever someone calls your victim, both you and the victim can pick it up and use the phone. Just mute yourself and listen in. Each brand of cell phone is different. Again, you will want to set this up with an anonymous debit card or use a phone company that does not require contracts or ID. You can also buy a used cell phone off the Internet and use that to create a clone.

This area of technology changes all the time so you will need to do your own research to figure out the latest thing.

COMPUTER HIJACKING

If you have not figured it out yet, your computer is not safe! If people really knew how easy it is to steal password or hijack their computer there would be massive panic and nobody would ever store personal information again. I am going to show you some very basic spy and hacking techniques that will get you oodles of information.

Computer hijacking is the most direct, easy and informative source by which to gain a victim's personal information. There are many ways to do this, depending on the type of access you can get to the victim's computer.

If you have physical access to their computer, you can get all their information surprisingly easily.

If they don't have any passwords to protect their operating system it's a breeze. You just need to be alone with the computer for a few minutes. You can surf around and see their history, or sometimes people save their email settings so when their browser opens, it automatically sings them in. If the victim uses instant messaging, they sometimes forget that when they hit the instant messaging icon, it can automatically sign you to the associated mail account too.

If you are in an office setting and on the same network, you can just go to your network settings and view their computer. You may have to know the name of the computer, but you can only see what they are doing at that particular time. Unfortunately, this is very limited and you have to be there to see what they are seeing. This would really only be worth it in an office situation.

If you need to bypass their first password that comes up when the computer boots up, you can type "admin" in the user name and no password. That will at least get you into an area where you can run a spy program. If that does not work, you can try using a recovery disc.

A recovery disc is a disc used to bypass unknown passwords. The idea of a recovery disc is if an employee acts out and changes the password when you fire them, or if you bought a used computer with a password you don't know, the recovery disc can get you around that. Network administrators stick in this disc and it bypasses the start up password and lets you make a new one. The one problem with this is you have to set a new password. This can be a big tip off to the victim that somebody is screwing with their computer, but most likely a victim will just blame it on the computer being crappy and old.

A much better and simpler way is to just invest in a good key logger program and install it on the victims computer. Key loggers are evil little programs that allow you to see everything your victim does. Parents secretly use key loggers on children all the time to see what their children are really doing when no one is watching them. I have also heard of children installing a key logger on their parents. They used the information to blackmail their parents into letting them do whatever they want and break the house rules. Nothing backs Mommy off like showing her a naughty chat log with a man who is not her husband. These are all things a good key logger should allow you to do.

Let's go through what you want in a good key logging program, one by one.

1. Stealth Monitoring- This means when the key logger is installed no search can find it.

2. Password capture- This allows you to get any name and password associated with that login.

3. Immune to Anti-Spy ware – Almost every computer has a spy ware protector on it. A good key logger will not be found, but they are usually the pricier ones.

4. Instant Messaging, webcam and microphone archiving - This will record both sides of an instant messaging conversation and all the webcam interactions and conversations. This feature alone is invaluable. Imagine not only getting the IM history but getting a webcam video of your victim, too. Think of all the perverted secrets you will have proof of. You want one that

> can be remotely installed and monitored. This means you can sneak this program in an email and trick your victim into opening it. It will act like a virus and you will be completely able to spy on your victim's computer from your home.

The world of key loggers changes every week, so you will want to do more of your own research for that.

So what to do if you cannot physically get to the victims computer?

Most of the Key logging programs can be snuck into an email and it will go to work. Simply set up an anonymous account like I said to do above and pretend to be one of the victim's trusted friend's who happens to be setting up a new email. Send a few friendly emails to build their trust and then attach a picture and the program, and say something like, "Hey, is this you in this picture?"

If you cannot get them to open an email with the hidden program you will have to hijack their network. You will have to get into the victim's wireless range, so just bring your laptop and park on the street. You need to do a little research to find the best program for this. Some programs that can break in are considered a password recovery tool for network administrators, but they can be used to steal passwords right out of the air. Basically, it works like an intermediary between a wireless network and a computer. A computer and the wireless network are always talking. It basically sticks itself in the middle of that process. Normally, a password goes straight from the victim's computer to the victim's wireless router. With some hacking programs the victim's password goes from the victim's computer to your computer then to the victim's wireless router.

Once you have the password, you can sign into the network and victim's computer and force it to open a key logger attached email. This will infect the victim's computer, and if you erase your installing activity, they will have no clue how it got there.

I cannot say this enough: once a good key logger program has infected your victim's computer, you can really dish out some serious revenge.

For more research on hacking into modems and computers search these terms.

"Code scanning", "break the encryption".

"Wireless packet sniffing"

"War Driving"

"Turbo encabulator"

Password ripping programs will automatically try every word in the dictionary to break a password. John the Ripper is my favorite.

TRACKING YOUR VICTIM

There are a few ways to do this depending on your budget. The cheapest is to stalk your victim and follow them around with a camera.

Another good way is to track them by GPS. If they have a cell phone with GPS capabilities, you can track them by their phone. In 2006, the government admitted to tracking people through their cell phones. The agents went so far as to turn them on without the owner's knowledge and listen in to their conversations. God bless this government and their helpful hand! You mean the government forgot to tell you they could do this to you without a warrant? Thank you again Patriot Act!

You can use the same technology to track people, too. You can look into a program called *"world tracker"* to get better information.

The other route is to actually plant a GPS tracker on somebody's car. They are small little black boxes that you can attach under the car. A warning, however; they are very pricey, ranging anywhere from about $300-$3000.

You can make a poor man's GPS tracker for less then $100 using this technique. The simplest way to use a GPS tracking service is to buy a prepaid phone that is GPS-enabled. You then need to subscribe to a GPS Locator service. You then have to plant the phone and recover it every few days. You will be able to use this service and get a complete time and record of your victim's whereabouts.

You can be even cheaper and track them for free. If you have your victim's cell phone information, and the victim's phone is GPS-enabled, you can sign them up for this service by pretending to be them. Remember earlier when I told you how to take over your victim's cell phone account? All you have to do is turn on something like parent tracker in the account. Then you can track the victim's phone with your computer. Unfortunately, the downside to this is the victim will know they are being tracked as soon as they get their next bill, so this might work for only one month, unless, of course, you change the address of the cell phone bill.

USING THE INTERNET

This might be obvious, but have you *Googled* your victim's name yet? You would be very surprised how easy it is to find out all about a person by typing in their name and variations of their name.

Did you get scammed or lied to about who a person really is, or where they really live? If you know their address or phone number, but not their real name, you can use a reverse listing service. Just search for them, there are free ones all over the net. You can also pay an information farm for their information if you have to. You can get everything from social security numbers to records of every thing they own. Collection agencies use information farms all the time to uncover hidden assets and attach judgments to properties. Just search the web for skip tracers and you will find a ton of the information farms.

If a person did you wrong and vanished, you can pay a skip tracer to locate them. They search for new utility bills, mailing addresses and things like that. You will have to be patient because it can take time for the person to resurface, but they always do eventually.

If you don't have time for these ideas, you can always just hire a local private investigator. It is truly amazing how fast a good private investigator can dig up dirt on somebody.

Have you ever had someone lie to you and say they never got your email? Well you can bust them with this great service www.readnotify.com. This service lets you mark the email secretly and sends proof of when the victim opened it. It even says where they open it from and what time. You might think you are doing business here only to find out the victim is in Nigeria. If you ever have to go to court, it is a great way to prove your victim is lying about not getting the email you sent them.

Don't forget about setting up a fake social networking account. You would not believe how many guys will add someone they don't know if they have a profile picture of a hot woman. Pretend to be a sexy man or woman on Twitter or Facebook and you can find out a ton of information on their comings and goings.

CHAPTER THREE:

THE LEGAL ROUTE

I really dislike the government and I believe they screw up anything they get involved with. They are completely incompetent when it comes to helping you get true justice. That may sound harsh, but wait until you're a victim of the system. Many people find out just what a mess this legal system is the first time they fall victim to a crime. You spend an enormous amount of time and money just trying to get justice, only to be rewarded with more paperwork. When you finally get some action, you find out that the predator has way more rights then the victim.

Don't believe me, talk to anybody who has ever been stalked. Basically the government can't really do anything to a stalker until after they have stabbed, shot or killed you.

Has anyone ever stolen from you or vandalized your property? First of all, it is almost impossible to prove it unless it is on film. Second, even if you can prove it, the police try their hardest to push it to civil court and not criminal. Once it is in civil court, it is a joke. Do you remember the OJ Simpson case? He had a massive civil judgment against him, yet he played golf everyday and enjoyed a wonderful lifestyle until he screwed up numerous times.

You see, even if you won a court case and tried to collect, it is damn near impossible if the person is a deadbeat who does not work or own assets on paper.

Ever had an underage person steal, vandalize or assault you? Underage predators almost always get just a slap on the wrist or a warning.

Ever try collecting child support? This is a legal maze of paperwork and frustration.

Let's just admit that government is pretty much useless to help you right a wrong and will probably compound the indignity you suffered.

You read all those reasons, but you still want to start with the legal route to get revenge or justice? Okay, I will give you a few examples of small victories I had when I tried to use the legal route.

I am no expert in legal advice, but I will share with you my experiences and victories.

I really hate deadbeats; they are the hardest people to get your money back from. They just openly steal from you or con you because they know there is very little you can do to them legally. In this chapter, I will be referring to anybody that's a deadbeat and screwed you over.

The first thing you need to know is that most of these crimes dance between a civil and a criminal charge. You want to try and persuade the bureaucrats to go criminal because it has much more bite. Unfortunately, it is decided by police and judges, on a whim, as to which way the case will be handled, criminal or civil. Most bureaucrats are very lazy and do not want to pursue criminal charges because it means much more work on their end.

The easiest way to nail someone criminally is if they write a bad check to you. Most people don't realize that a bad check can get them in very hot water and they can end up in jail quickly.

Back when I used to own rental properties inevitably somebody would owe me money and poor mouth about how they did not have it. I insisted they at least write a check and I would hold it until they paid me what was due.

The person who owed me would write me a check and I would sit on it for a little bit. Do not let them post date the check, which is illegal in many states. Make them date it for that day and tell them you will not deposit it until they tell you to. If they jerked me around at all about paying me back, I would deposit the check, knowing it would bounce.

The end result is now I had a bounced check, which is criminal offense instead of civil offense. The deadbeat would find out that I was holding something over their head that had some teeth to it. Once they find out they could go to jail, they will usually cough up the money. So when dealing with deadbeats, you want to set them up so they will bounce a check to you.

This technique also works against deadbeat spouses who write bad child support checks. Just hold the check and set them up so it will bounce. When people are living paycheck to paycheck, you want to hold the check and deposit between pay periods when you know they are stretching their bills.

Another great thing you can do with bounced checks is resubmit them. Very few people realize they can deposit them again. Most of the time the bad check will have a stamp on it that says do not resubmit. This is merely a suggestion and you can absolutely resubmit and the deadbeat won't be expecting it.

The best way to handle it is to wait until the beginning of the month. Most people on government funds get their checks at the very beginning of the month. Start calling the bank where the check is written from and tell the teller this. Say, "I am a merchant and (the deadbeat's name) just wrote me a check for $$$$ amount. Before I accept it, I would like to know if there is enough in the account to honor it." If the bank says no, call every day, and as soon as they say, "Yes, the check is good," go to that bank immediately and present the bad check to be cashed. That will clean out the deadbeat's account and you will get your money.

This little trick has gotten me back a lot of money from people who swore I would never get a dime out of them. I have been patient and in some cases it took me months of checking until they deposited the money. The best part about it is the deadbeat usually does not know about it until it is too late and their checks are bouncing all over the place and they are racking up a bunch of bank charges. It is a sweet karmic payback.

Okay, so what do you do if you can't trick them into writing a bad check? Unfortunately, you will have to sue them civilly. Something I found out in my adventures in legal land is that when you have to sue, go for all the money. Don't forget to include court costs, an hourly rate your time cost for dealing with this, travel expenses, reimbursement for time off work, and ask for punitive damages, too. Most of the time judges will say no, but if the deadbeats don't even show up, the judge will give you everything you ask for.

Another thing is, if you have to sue somebody, sue everybody. The more names you can get on a judgment the better and easier it is to collect. So when you have to sue put the business name, the father, mother and child. Now it is the deadbeat's responsibility in court to remove the names that are not involved. In my experience, only about 1 out of 5 deadbeats will even show to court. So you will get a default judgment with everyone's name on it. This will make collecting the money much easier.

Okay, hopefully now you've gotten a nice sized judgment. How do you collect? This can be hard, but there are a few ways to go about it.

If you are sick of dealing with this at this point use a collection agency. I love this one collection agency called www.sakalcai.com. They are great and take care of everything. If you want to do it yourself, keep reading.

Send a letter demanding garnishment of wages and a copy of your judgment to their boss. Deadbeats HATE this because it looks very poor in the work place and embarrasses the hell out of them. Make sure to send letters to everyone's bosses you got a judgment against and embarrass the whole lot of them. Usually that works and you will get checks until they are paid up.

If they don't have a job, it is harder to collect but not impossible. What you have to do is talk a cop into helping you. Take the judgment over to the police station and literally beg every cop you see to help you collect it. Asking police to help you is humiliating, I know, but how desperate are you to get your money back? This is the hardest part because most of police are way too lazy and don't want to do this. I had to basically bribe one to do this for me by giving him a cut. Some cops really are corrupt by the way, if you did not know.

Once you've got a cop on board, you can go to the victim's bank and empty their accounts. If they do not have an account then you get to be really mean.

You need to talk the cop into taking their possessions and selling them off to pay you. First, check the tax records to see if they own any cars. If they own cars that are free of liens, you're in business. The cop will impound and auction the cars to get your money back.

If they are truly deadbeats in every sense of the word, then they won't have a checking account or a lien free car. The cop will actually go and remove and sell their possessions, until the debt is paid.

Before the cop will go to seize possessions, you have to list everything you can think of that they own. The cops can only take the possessions you write down on the list. If you're lucky, you might have been in their house and remember what you saw.

Most likely you really have no clue what they own so you will have to guess. Almost all people have these things so you can use my list here.

Computers, Ipads, smart phones, mp3 players, printers, scanners, gaming systems like xbox or play station and the games that go with them.

Couches, sofa, furniture;

Kitchen table and chairs;

TVs, vcr, dvr, cd and dvd players;

Stereo, boom box, music cds and dvds;

Their computers (they will try and say that the computers belong to the kids and not them). If you sued everyone in the family then you can take everything. If not, take the computers that are not in their kid's room;

Mattresses, sheets, comforters, pillows and window dressings;

All their clothes and jewelry;

All kitchen cookware, silverware and knives;

Guns and Firearms (because I remembered this one, I literally made all my money back when the cops sold one victim's antique gun collection);

Coins and stamps;

Picture frames on wall (this really pisses them off that you would sell their family pictures for pennies);

Cosmetics and make up (some women will have hundreds of dollars of stuff, although you won't be able to sell these for much it will really piss them off).

Just understand the deadbeat thinks they are untouchable and when you completely clean them out so they have no clothes, no beds and can't even brush their teeth they are going to hate you.

I have done this a few times to deadbeats who stole from me and didn't miss a wink of sleep over it. Remember -- I never strike first, I only strike back. These people stole money from me first by either skipping out of a bill or not paying me rent for 3 months, situations like that. I feel it is even justice because of all the time and money I wasted dealing with their unethical actions.

So, if you're going to see it all the way through to end of the legal mess, don't just strike back, strike back hard!

Since we are on the topic of the legal route, we need to address one of the best things about the legal mess.

One of the best forms of revenge is to use the mindless bureaucracy of government to your advantage. Force your victim to deal with the huge government machine and make them waste their time and money. You can use the court system's ineptness against your revenge victim. Let me explain what I mean.

A good example of this comes from the divorce experience of one of my best friends. He was separated and his wife took their child, mainly for the child support check. He really wanted his kid to be with him, but lets face it the American legal system is very unfair to men in divorce cases. She was awarded the child and alimony.

The ex-wife would lie to the son and say his father wasn't paying her child support and that his father was always screwing her over.

The son told the father what the mother said and he was furious. He fixed the situation by signing all the checks in both the mother and child's name.

The ex-wife was pissed off to no end the first time she went to cash the check and the bank refused to cash the child support check without the son there to sign his name too. She actually had to go pull him out of school and take him to the bank. Too funny!

Anyway, he got sick of her and offered to buy her out in one lump payment. She accepted with the understanding that there would be no more payments ever. The opportunist was a 1st class deadbeat and spent all the money on her that was supposed to be for the child, The succubus was completely broke in a matter of months. The ex-wife hired an attorney to draft a letter demanding more money.

This is where my friend was brilliant, using the legal system against her to clean her out. The wife would have to pay $250 every time her lawyer had to write a letter. When my friend got the letter, he said he didn't understand and asked for a further explanation of some of the legal definitions.

The letter would go back to her lawyer; he would revise it and send another demand letter to the tune of another $250.

My friend did this and kept slowly negotiating one change at a time and dragged the letters out for months. Each time the succubus's lawyer would revise the letter, he charged her $250. After paying a few thousand dollars for legal fees, she just ran out of money and gave up. She could no longer afford to hire the attorney and he eventually turned on her and sued her for all the letter drafting fees.

Another way to bankrupt someone for revenge is to just keep suing someone. As long as you don't spend money on a lawyer and they do, they will waste thousands of dollars. I learned this the hard way. I had a patient threaten to sue me over a few dollars. It dragged out and became a huge legal mess just to mount a defense. Even though nothing ever happened and I never went to court, it cost me $10,000 to defend it. That guy got revenge on me big time.

There are just so many ways to use the government against someone that I will give many examples in another chapter. Most of the time when someone goes to court it is because a bureaucrat is threatening the person with fines and jail time. So I rather enjoy using the system to defend myself against those who make a living off victims of the system.

If you need to get revenge against the system or bureaucrats, there are some great ideas for that, too.

I really like Marc Stevens approach to handling bureaucrats. He has saved people hundreds of years in jail and hundreds of thousands of dollars.

This site is also a good place to find out how people have dealt with B.S. lawsuits. www.adventuresinlegalland.com.

CHAPTER FOUR

VERY NASTY REVENGE IDEAS

Now you should be patient and gather as much information as you can. If you just wait long enough, the victim will provide some information to hang themselves. You need to take your time and plan your revenge well. Let your victim feel that they got away with screwing you and there is nothing you can do about it.

The predator is a bad person and will have probably also screwed some other people over by then. Sadly, they probably conned many good folks before they got to you. As time goes by it will build confusion and doubt because the predator will not really know which of his many victims is attacking him.

By this time, you have at least the victim's real name and address. You have dug through their trash, and have installed a key logger to see what they have been doing. The next ideas will be mean, nasty but not life destroying. I am saving those gems for the end for this book.

THE VICTIM – NOW A VICTIM OF FRAUD

For this revenge idea you will need:

A randomly used computer purchased anonymously

Your identity guarded by hiding your IP Address

Surf on the net by anonymously using something like Startpage

A new email account (anything like Gmail, Yahoo, Thunderbird)

A hushmail account

A random wireless hotspot (like a coffee shop or some fast food joints)

The victim's name, social security # and financial info, etc.

Here is how this payback works. First, protect yourself using the ideas above and do them in that order.

You need to put up a few random advertisements all over a free internet classifed site like Craigslist. Make the ad for the most popular electronics as bait for scam artists. Say something like, "I have a few new Iphones and Ipads that I need to sell cheap. I can even take payments which are cardable."

What will happen is you will get a ton of emails from legitimate people who want to buy the I-phone, just ignore those. The word cardable is a code word to internet thieves that tells them you will take their credit card payment with no questions asked.

What you're looking for is anyone who wants to offer you more money then you ask for and then mail you a cashier's check. Those guys are total scam artists. You will also be on the lookout for anyone from overseas, especially somebody from Nigeria. This is where www.readnotify.com is very helpful. You want to find people overseas looking who want to buy your I-Phone (or whatever the hottest electronic is).

Just keep re-listing advertisements until you get about 10 scam artist's email addresses. Then you will want to send out this email, using the tips I gave you earlier to stay anonymous.

Dear [victim's name],

I just wanted to confirm all your information before completing your order.

Name,

Address,

SS#

Credit card #

Checking account number

Please let me know where you want your phones shipped?

Then send this to your entire scam artist email list, one at a time, so the scam artist believes you only sent it to them individually.

Wait a few hours and send this follow up letter.

*****

To whom it may concern,

A private invoice email was accidentally sent to your address instead of our buyer. Please ignore the last email and destroy that information.

Your attention to this matter would be much appreciated.

Thank you

*****

Now if you have emailed out 10 scam artists, 2-3 of them will fall for this and steal the information. They will take it and sell it on underground chat forums which are set up to sell stolen identification. Within a few hours the victim's information will be cloned and their accounts will be emptied by crooks.

Once a victim of identity theft, the victim will have problems for years to come. The extra bonus is that criminals will attack them for years and it is super frustrating to deal with.

You can also make sure their information finds its way to all the wrong people by stamping all the victims personal information on dollar bills. Just spend enough of them and eventually they will find there way to some crooks.

This is an evil payback but it is a great way to get even with someone who stole all your money or cleaned you out.

YOUR VICTIM HAS BAD CREDIT

You will want to find as many credit card applications as you can get.

Find a mailbox drop way outside your zip code.

Wear gloves and don't use your handwriting or better yet type the applications

You can also do them online if you follow all these steps. You will need:

A random, used computer purchased anonymously

Your identity guarded by hiding your IP Address

Surf on the net anonymously using something like Startpage

A new email account (anything like Gmail, Yahoo, Thunderbird)

A hushmail account

A random wireless hotspot (like a coffee shop or some fast food joints)

Anonymously, apply for the victims for as many cards as possible. Trash the application so the person won't be accepted. Put that the victim only makes like $10,000 a year and is unemployed. Every time you apply and they are rejected it is a black mark on their credit. Due this long enough and it will trash their credit.

YOUR VICTIM IS A CHEAT

Want to break up your victim's marriage or relationship? Make sure they deserve this, only use this in self-defense. Nothing is as vicious as causing a divorce or a nasty breakup. It is emotionally and financially draining. Here is what you will need first:

A randomly used computer purchased anonymously

Your identity guarded by hiding your IP Address

Surf on the net anonymously

A new email account (anything like Gmail, Yahoo, Thunderbird)

A hushmail account

A random wireless hotspot (like a coffee shop or some fast food joints)

Spouse's or lovers name and email address.

This might take some real work, depending on how loyal the victim's spouse or partner is, but eventually, if you can plant enough mistrust for a long enough period of time, it will do an amazing amount of damage to the marriage or relationship.

First, use all the preparation ideas above to ensure your complete anonymity.

Now you will start by creating a profile on a free dating site. You can use www.plentyoffish.com so there is no money trail leading to you.

Create a perverted sex oriented profile in your victim's name, make sure you mention you are married but you hate your spouse because they are such an awful lover and person. Make sure to include a good photo of your victim.

Now you want to also make a fake sex crazed site for your victim's new lover. Make up a real slut! Have fun with the site and even make the fake person into some really gross stuff.

Next send an email from the fake victim's profile to the fake lover's profile and have them start a juicy affair. If you know the victim well enough and know his or her schedule, then plan the emails around those times. Perhaps your victim is leaving for a work trip. Have a string of emails between the two fake profiles. Have them plan a secret sex rendezvous when you know your victim is leaving town. A good way to find this out is to create a fake social networking account like on twitter or Facebook. You will easily be able to figure out whenever the victim left on a work trip.

In your emails have the victim ask for no phone calls ever and to talk only by email. Have the victim say it is too dangerous to call each other at the victim's house or cell, "lets just use email." This will be important later when the spouse checks the phone records and finds nothing.

Keep this going for a while, really build up a relationship, and start flirting like crazy to anyone interested in your fake victim's profile. Reply to any profiles that are interested in your victim and start flirting.

You have now built a nice bit of proof for the spouse. We need much more.

The art of a good photo editor can cause fantastic damage. You need to do a quality job and cut a picture of the victim and the fake lover together. A sex picture is even better, but could be very hard to edit well.

Also, get a picture of some flowers or a cookie basket the victim sent your fake lover. Email a picture and say, "I love the flowers or cookies you sent me; here is what they look like. Thanks. I hope you remembered to use cash so your spouse or lover won't find out."

If you really have time make multiple lovers for your victim.

You now want your target and their fake lover to start fighting. Have the victim say he will be asking for a divorce in the next few weeks so he can get married to the fake lover. Have the fake lover say, "If you won't ask for a divorce, I will spill the beans about us."

Have a nasty fight go down.

Send an email to the victim's spouse saying, "I know you don't know me, but I know you. I have been dating your spouse secretly and I am tired of all the sneaking around. The victim told me if I told you, that he would act like he has no idea who I am."

"Here is some proof, I met your spouse on this website, and here is the profile. Take a look!"

"Here are a few of our emails if you don't believe me. I also have a few pictures."

Forward all the fake conversations and website address. You can always save the pictures for later if case you need more proof.

Now sit back and enjoy the fireworks. Keep openly antagonizing the situation and refuse to meet, claiming you fear for your safety. Say you're also done with the victim and you don't want to see them again because the target had many other affairs that you just found out about.

Now, hopefully, you have saved all the information about the people who emailed your victims profile. Give out the victim's number to them and ask them to call when you think the spouse will be there.

Having strange people calling and asking for the victim should flame the fires of distrust. There is only so much a spouse will believe before they think the victim is totally lying to them.

Just keep it going by sending gifts to the house from different people and place some ads on *www.craigslist.com* with the victim's phone number.

If you have access, plant a strategic pair of panties or a pack of condoms in the victim's car for the spouse to find.

This one is great if you can pull it off. Follow the victim and spouse to the store. While they are in the store, leave a note that says something like this:

"Hey baby, I saw your car and wanted to say hi! Call me to confirm we are still on for our lunch tomorrow. Xoxoxoxo!"

Call a local radio station and make a sappy love song request from the victim to the fake lover. This works great if you know the spouse's workplace plays a certain radio station all day long. Rumors will get around the office quickly and the embarrassed spouse will be furious.

Use your anonymous phone and email to hire some hookers from Craigslist to come over and ask for your victim. You will find the hookers under "services," then choose "erotic." You will see tons of ads for "massages."

You are looking for one who will do an outbound call. When you call, just talk about the massage and don't approach them for sex or they will think you're a cop and not show up. If you are really lucky, you WILL call an undercover cop and the victim will get blamed.

Send a package to the victim's house with earrings or a watch in it. Attach this note.

"Dear [Victim],

This was found in your room and we tracked you down by your bill. Thanks for staying with us and we appreciate all your business.

Thank You,

(any shady hotel's name)

Make sure not to put the victim's name on the package so the spouse will open it and find the letter and trinket. Also, do not mention the day the victim stayed at the hotel, just leave it open ended so the victim won't have a clear alibi.

Book a hotel room through a travel agent for your victim and fake lover. Tell the agent you do not have an email and to please send the bill and confirmation by mail to your victim's house. Make sure they put both the name of the victim and the fake lover on the envelope.

Really put the nail in the coffin of your victim by arranging a fake marriage. Use your fake lover and the victim, and send in a wedding announcement to the local paper.

You will need a partner to be the fake lover and you pretend to be the victim. Set up a church, reception hall, band, cake, the whole works. Make sure you use all the services you can that will bill you later and rack up a huge bill.

Then don't show up and let all the businesses demand payment from the victim. Make sure all the businesses got the victim's address and credit card numbers. If you are lucky, you will get a bonus if the spouse opens the bills for the wedding.

Send a fake divorce notice to appear in court to the victim's spouse.

These revenge ideas take a lot of work but can really drive the nail into the coffin if the victim has a shaky relationship to start with. Most likely if the victim was unethical screwing you over, then they are probably being unethical to their spouse or partner as well and you are doing them a favor.

YOUR VICTIM KNOCKS UP FAKE LOVER

Why not involve your victim's family? If the victim is a male, send their parents a letter from your fake lover saying that their son got you pregnant and he is blackmailing you into getting an abortion. If it is a female, say she is blackmailing you to get money for an abortion and you thought her parents should know.

YOUR VICTIM HAS A VENEREAL DISEASE

Follow up the prank above by having your fake lover call the county health department and report that the victim has a V.D. Say the victim lied about having a V.D. and gave it to you on purpose. Most of the time, the health department is forced to open an investigation on the victim. They will go to their house and ask the victim very intrusive questions. If you are lucky, their spouse or lover will want to know what this is all about and it will cause more distrust.

This works really great if you make a fake test result from a lab and send it to the health department. While you're at it, you might as well send the fake test to the victim's house for the spouse to find.

YOUR VICTIM THE CHILD MOLESTER

This one can ruin somebody's career and their life. Have you ever seen those "To Catch a Predator" shows. If you have not, this is what happens in the show. Basically, some pervert meets what he thinks is a kid on the Internet and entices them to meet up for sex. The show entraps the predator and then sets them up at a house where they are to be filmed. When the predator shows up, the cops jump out and arrest the predator.

For this revenge idea you will need:

A randomly used computer purchased anonymously

Your identity guarded by hiding your IP Address anonymously

A new email account (anything like Gmail, Yahoo, Thunderbird)

A hushmail account

A random wireless hotspot (like a coffee shop or some fast food joints). Do not go anywhere where you're on film, stay out in your car if you have to, and cover up your vehicle license plate.

Victim's personal information:

You REALLY need to remain anonymous for this one or you will end up in jail. The cops don't screw around when it comes to child porn and this is very high risk. I would advise against even thinking about using this one.

You will want to go to some chat rooms posing as your victim. Start chatting it up with some underage kids and making some underage friends.

What you need to realize is the new anti-predator laws are extremely powerful. You can go to jail just by talking to an underage kid. You don't even have to meet with them; all you have to do is send them adult information online.

These chat rooms are loaded with cops pretending to be kids. If your ID is hidden by the steps above you should be in the clear. Start chatting and try to find the cops. Simply invite them to your victim's house, if they are cops they will try and get you to go to their sting house, don't fall for it. If you talk to enough people you will stumble on a cop pretending.

The cops don't play around with child predators. Even if you never do anything but act suspicious, the police go to the victim's house and arrest them. It does not matter if they find them guilty or not. It will make a mess out of the victim's life. When rumor gets out they are a child predator they will lose their job, their life, and be ostracized by their community. It does not matter when they are found innocent, the damage will have already been done.

A good way to get your victim unwanted attention is to put an advertisement on *www.craigslist.com* like this one. "I am looking for young boys and girls to model in artistic poses, great pay for discrete clients. Please mention the ad when you call..." Put your victim's spouse's phone number and their work's receptionist's phone number.

Another good way to make them into sex predators is to make a copycat webpage of the national sexual predator registry. Copy the local page and make a fake version of it. Copy the predators and add your victim's picture and name to the list. Anonymously email their co-workers and neighbors the link to the fake page.

Leave a phone message on the victim's spouse's phone and say, "This is Mr. Jones and I am very excited about getting together tomorrow to look at these pictures of your little cutie. I am bringing cash and am willing to double the amount if you can bring the little cutie to our meeting." Use a voice changer and an anonymous phone.

Another way that is much more risky is to pay an anonymous child to say he was molested by the victim. You really need to be careful to protect your identity and it is best not to set this up with the kid face to face.

Children have openly lied about their teachers or parents molesting them just to get them in trouble. The victim always gets suspended while they investigate. When the victim is finally cleared, it is too late and their reputation and career is ruined. Of course, nothing ever happens to the lying child and they are above the law.

If you get lucky, the cops won't believe them and it will drag on for years.

THE VICTIM LIVES IN THE STONE AGE

Make the victim see what it was like to live in the Stone Age. Before you do this make sure you are paying back the entire family who wronged you. You're a real jerk if you screw with the victim's family if they are innocent.

For this revenge Idea you will need:

Anonymous phone number like Skype or an old fashioned pay phone or prepaid cell with a fake name.

All the victims' utilities and financial bills

Voice modification or a good disguise voice

The way this one works is you will want to use an anonymous phone and to call your victim's utility companies. Wait until you know your victim is leaving town for a few days, then strike hard. You can also set everything to go off Friday evening because they won't get anyone to come out and turn it back on until Monday.

Call and cancel their electric service first. When the power goes out, it will cause their food to rot and ruin their fridge.

Cancel their gas. If this is done during the winter you could get lucky and cause a couple of pipes to burst.

Then cancel their water. Nothing is as inconvenient as not having water. Your victim returns from vacation, only to find out they can't use their toilet or shower.

Cancel their Satellite or cable, internet and phone.

Cancel their trash service. This is fun because it can take a few weeks before the trash company works them back into rotation.

Cancel their auto, health and life insurance.

Finally cancel their cell phone. If you are lucky, they will be nailed with a huge fine for cancelling their contract.

Don't forget to cancel all their credit cards, too. Hopefully this will ruin their vacation and possibly screw up their return trip.

YOUR VICTIM ABUSES HIS OR HER SPOUSE

This is a fun rumor to start and can really cause problems for your victim.

For this revenge Idea you will need:

Anonymous phone number like Skype or an old fashion pay phone

You can also use an old random cell phone or a prepaid phone with a fake name.

You can take an old cell phone or use an untraceable phone to make the call. Old cell phones can always call 911 even if they don't have any service to them. Just make sure you use one that has nothing to do with you and was never in your name. You will also want to handle the cell phone with gloves. Most cell phones can be tracked so you will want to throw it into a river or destroy it completely after your finished making the call. Also you want to use a fake voice or a voice modulator.

Just say you were near the property and heard the husband beating the wife. He screamed he would kill her. The cops always have to come out and investigate these calls and make a report.

Make one of these calls every few days. Should be fun to see watch all the neighbors show up and be nosey. Your victim will also start to rack up a fine record of complaints.

YOUR VICTIM NEEDS TO BUILD AN ARC

This is a nasty way to ruin your victim's house.

You will need:

Gloves

Hose

Shovel

This revenge idea works best under the cover of night. You will want to wear gloves so there are no finger prints to track.

Wait for your victim to leave on vacation or on business for a few days. Sneak over at night and screw a hose to the outside spigot. Either open a window or break one. Stick the hose deep into the house and turn it on. Try to pick a window that cannot be seen easily, like behind a bush or tree. You also want to pick a spigot that the victim's neighbors will not see easily.

After a few days of flooding, the wood floors will be warped or carpet ruined. The level below will be ruined as well. The most damage will be the widespread mold that will quickly grow in the wall and floors.

As a final slap in the face, the homeowner will get an enormous water bill.

This is very, very destructive payback idea and should only be used on someone who is a horrible person and has done equal damage to you.

THERE GOES THE VICTIM'S NEIGHBORHOOD

You will need a mailbox which is not in your zip code.

You will also need the names and addresses of a few neighbors (use the reverse directory to get this info)

Type out an official looking letter from a pest control company. The letter should say that your victim's address is the site of massive termite and cockroach infestation. By law, a homeowner is required to make the local neighbors aware of this infestation so they can test their own houses. If the neighbor finds any infestation at their house, the victim is responsible for all costs to treat the infestation.

Your neighbors will treat the victim like the plague and, if by dumb luck the neighbor does have termites, they will blame the victim and try to get them to pay. This will make the victim very uncomfortable in his own neighborhood and might even affect the resale value of his house.

You can make this funnier by planting bugs in the victim's house and their neighbor's houses. You can buy roaches at some pet stores and poke them through a window screen or dryer vent.

YOU'RE THE VICTIM AND THE POLICE

These are fun ways to get the police to pull the victim over.

For this revenge Idea you will need:

Anonymous phone number like Skype or an old fashioned pay phone or a prepaid phone in a fake name.

Voice modification or a good disguise voice

This revenge idea works best in the cover of night. You will want to wear gloves so there are no finger prints to track.

The easiest way to get the victim pulled over is to just steal their license plate. I mean, who really checks to see if they have a license plate on their car everyday. It will only take a few days and they will eventually be pulled over.

The best time to do steal the plate is when your victim goes out to a bar. If you are lucky, not only will they get pulled over but they could get a DWI, too. To help get them a DWI, call the cops and say you suspect they are drunk because they almost ran in to you. Make sure you cancel the victim's insurance before you do this so they get fined for driving uninsured, too.

Get them in major trouble by planting drugs in the car first. Make sure to put enough to make it a serious enough crime to go to jail for.

Or make an anonymous call to the police and report the car stolen, then steal the plate. Eventually, they will be pulled over and have to explain why they are driving a stolen car. If you are lucky the cops will yank them out of the car and ask questions later. You can always count on the cops to overreact when they pull somebody over.

You can also use bumper stickers that say "I hate cops," or "I love cop killers".

You can drop of a bunch of pornographic magazines and books at the local elementary schools library. Drop the pornographic magazines and pornographic books off and leave a typed note asking that the school please send a record of the donation to the victims address for taxes. The school will most likely turn this over to the cops and they will investigate your victim.

Another good payback idea is to search the FBI most wanted list and find somebody that looks like your victim. Send an anonymous tip that you think they are hiding out using your victims name as an alias.

You will also want to tip off all the local bounty hunters to this tidbit of information. Bounty hunters are high adrenaline macho meatheads that will go after the victim without really checking it out too deeply. If you can find someone who has a really large bounty that looks like your victim, the bounty hunters will not waste time with too much research and will just bust the victim.

Make a bunch of anonymous calls and threaten people. Be sure to give out your victim's name when you threaten people. A better way is to use a caller ID spoofer and to make your victim's name and phone number appear when you threaten them.

If you get lucky enough, you will call a psycho and stir them up so they will go to your victim's house looking for revenge.

Another fun way is to plant drugs in the victim's garage and then make an anonymous call to the police that you saw him selling and dealing drugs out of his garage to some underage kids.

YOUR VICTIM IS SO CHARITABLE

For this revenge Idea you will need:

Anonymous phone number like Skype or an old fashion pay phone or a prepaid phone in a fake name

Voice modification or a good disguise voice

Call your local Kidney Foundation, Salvation Army, or any charity that people put out pick ups for. Tell the charity that you saw the victim's car and license plate number steal all the pick up items.

Or you can donate your victim's car to the National Kidney Foundation. Ask them to pick it up when the victim is on vacation. Just say "Sorry, I lost the title, but I will mail it when I get a new one. Can you guys just come and tow it away please?"

If you have your victim's credit card number, make a huge donation while you are at it. The victim will look like a real jerk taking money back from orphans. This would also work just if you called and pledged money at every local charity you can think of with your victim's info. Make the victim look like a huge ass when they stand up the local Girl Scout troop.

You can also use the victim's employer and pledge a bunch of donations to the community. When the local Little League shows up for their check, your victim will get in major trouble at work for pledging all the donations in the company's name.

If you know your victim orders Christmas gifts by mail, then use a change of address form and send it to your favorite charity. When the charity see gifts arrive, they will assume they are donations.

KILL YOUR VICTIM

Place an Obituary in the paper you know the victim reads. Place the ad on a Saturday morning. Anonymously spread a rumor that the victim died in an email to the victim's co-workers, and send a link to the article in the paper.

Obtain a blank death certificate and fill it out in your victim's name. Send it to as many government agencies as possible. You definitely want to make sure you send it to the social security office and the victim's financial institutions. If the government and banks think the victim is dead they will freeze the accounts for the probation process. Make sure to kill your victim on paper every year.

This will cause a huge headache and the jerk will be buried by paperwork just trying to prove he's alive. Because of the Social Security Department's incompetence, they will continue to let you kill the victim over and over. This is a very nasty revenge idea that could possibly screw with the victim for the rest of their life.

Call a local funeral home and the victim's pastor and ask them to send someone over to the victim's house to discuss burial arrangements with their spouse.

HELP YOUR VICTIM WITH THEIR CURB APPEAL

Anonymous phone numbers like Skype or an old fashion pay phone or a prepaid phone in a fake name

Voice modification or a good disguise voice

A good disguise and fake license plate

Wait for your victim to leave on holiday and set up some construction to be done. Make sure you use a fake license plate and a good disguise.

First, call a septic company and tell them your tank needs to be cleaned. Tell them you are not sure where the tank is. Give them about 5-6 areas to try where you think the tank is. Of course, make sure one of those areas is in the flower bed.

While this is going on, have some yard workers show up to remove the bushes and small trees. I suggest you find these guys on *www.craigslist.com,* using an anonymous email and phone. If you are feeling very mean, have them remove the grass in an area and cut down a tree.

Make sure that you order a few truckloads of gravel to be dumped in their lawn. Just tell them you need to make a large parking space for the new RV you're buying. Make sure the new parking pad is right in the center of their lawn.

Order a large pile of manure to be dumped inside the victim's car port, driveway or garage.

Transplant kudzu vines into your victim's yard. Once this stuff takes root, it is almost impossible to get rid of.

Don't forget to plant some marijuana seeds on the back side of the property. They will be so busy cleaning this mess up that they won't notice the pot growing. This would be great payback for DEA agents and judges. Wait a week or two and make an anonymous tip off to the paper. "Local DEA agent grows the best pot, pictures on page five."

Wait for the yard demolition to get started and tell them you need to run up to the store for a few minutes. Drive off and don't look back.

The workers will finish tearing the hell out of the yard and wait around to be paid. When they are not paid they will keep showing up and coming around until they are. Your victim might even get sued for the labor cost for the destruction of his own yard. The jerk will actually have to pay for the services eventually.

YOUR VICTIM WILL NEVER GET TO SLEEP IN AGAIN

Anonymous phone number like Skype or an old fashion pay phone or a prepaid phone in a fake name

Voice modification or a good disguise voice

A random used computer purchased anonymously

Your identity guarded by hiding your IP Address

Surf on the net anonymously.

A new email account (anything like Gmail, Yahoo, Thunderbird)

A hushmail account

A random wireless hotspot (like a coffee shop or some fast food joints)

You will want to use your anonymous phone and email and help your victim sell their house. They want to move, they just don't know it yet.

You want to start by taking photos and listing their house on www.craiglist.com. Make the advertisement for the house look great and ask a ridiculous low price. Say you have to sell your house immediately because you are trying to avoid foreclosure. Set up a very early open house and say "cash talks, first buyer there with cash gets the house at this low price. Bids start at 6am this Saturday morning." Don't leave a phone number and do put the address in. Do this every week.

Next week call all the "stop foreclosure ads" you can find. Drive around and get them from all the little signs at intersections. Also check the papers and Internet for these types of ads. Call them all and ask them to come over and discuss their proposition. Make yourself sound desperate and tell them you need to sell fast.

The people that run these rescue from foreclosure outfits are ripe with corruption and scams. These people will relentlessly hassle the victim and will not take no for an answer.

The next attack you will want to do is to call all the realtors in town and ask them to come over and take a look at the house. Set up appointments nice and early on weekdays so the victim never gets to sleep late any day.

While you are at it you might as well invite every insurance sales person to your victim's house to discuss buying insurance.

Invite some in home salesman like Kirby vacuum cleaners, gutter salesman and home improvement salespeople.

One of the best groups to annoy your victim with is the Mormons. Go on the web and search around www.lds.com until you find the page that allows you to request a home visit. Make sure you request it nice and early.

Be sure to remember to report a massive gas leak at your victim's house. Call in the leak in the middle of the night.

Call the police late at night and say that you saw a masked figure trying to break into your victim's house.

Organize a political rally at your victim's house nice and early. Put an anonymous advertisement out to support the troops or rally against fur. Make sure you say it will go on all day long and it is all you can eat with free beer and wine.

Between all these groups of people, your victim will be held hostage in their own house. If you keep this going for months, the victim will never answer the door again and never get to sleep late either. They might get so fed up that they will move.

YOUR VICTIM GOES TO COURT

We talked about simply suing a victim over and over to cost them ridiculous legal fees, but unfortunately, that does not follow my advice about staying anonymous. Let me give you some other stealthier ideas.

Get online and download some examples of legal forms. You can find legal notices like judgments, summonses, condemnations, code violations, search and arrest warrants. Download the forms and alter them with your victim's information. Send summonses to the victim's home and set a fake court date. The victim will have no idea what this is about and spend money on legal counsel. It will take the victim a while to discover that this notice is fake.

You can also send a fake judgment to the victim's boss demanding garnishment of wages. Have the judgment say the victim is being garnished because they committed fraud and embezzlement at their last job. Have the court ordered money go to a charity like the Humane Society, or something similar.

Another great way to use the fake judgments is to turn them over to a collection agency. They are relentless and will never believe the victim does not really owe money. One of the best ways to use a fake judgment is to make one for fake child support. Turn the judgment over to the special collection agencies that go after deadbeat dads. The laws are very harsh when it comes to collecting child support and the agency can really make your victim squirm.

Eventually they will figure out it is a fake judgment, but by the time they do, you will be long gone and the damage to victim will already be done.

If you think we live in a Republic where you are innocent until proven guilty, you are kidding yourself. When you attack someone using government agencies like this, they will always be treated as if they are guilty and the victim will have to prove they are innocent. This will take a huge amount of time and money, and create a whole lot of stress in your victim's life.

YOUR VICTIM IS RACIST

This is a fun way to destroy your victim's reputation and business creditability.

Write an editorial response to a local paper. Pick a very unpopular position and submit a very racist response. Have some fun with it and make your victim sound crazy. This also works well on social websites. You might want to even get the attention of the authorities by taking a pro-terrorist stance or anti-police stance. Be sure to include their name, address and phone number, and challenge any reader who disagrees to contact them.

You can also disguise your voice and use an anonymous phone to call a talk show. Make sure you mention the victims name and where they work as much as possible while you spew racist remarks on the show. Also make sure you mention that everyone where the victim works feels the same way they do. The victim's work will have to fire him to save face and show the public they are not racist.

Set up a meeting for the Klan, Black Panthers, or other racist organizations at the victim's house. Make sure you include the victim's name and address in the advertisement. Don't forget to offer free beers and pizza.

YOUR VICTIM IS A STALKER

Why not send love letters from the victim to their co-workers. Have the letters start getting sexual and let the co-worker know that you really enjoy watching them at work. While you're at it have your victim stalk another victim you don't like. Just spy on them and send letters about how attractive you thought their last outfit was and how you also liked what they wore at the gym.

Start sending two to three letters a day to their work from your victim and have them get creepier and creepier. If you're lucky, they will take out a restraining order against your target.

Drop the victim's work card outside the window of the stalked victim. You can also plant some video tape wrappers so it looks like they opened a new tape outside the stalked victim's window.

Slip a note under the stalked victim's door saying, "I am watching, you are so beautiful". Also place this note on their car and at their work.

Take some long distance surveillance pictures and mail them to the stalked. Carelessly leave your victims address on the envelope.

Judges will give a TRO or restraining order very easily because they don't want to get in trouble if the stalker kills somebody. It is surprisingly easy to get a restraining order even without any real evidence because the judges cover their butts.

YOUR VICTIM IS AN ILLEGAL ALIEN

If your victim is a minority this will be much easier. Just make an anonymous tip to any immigration or ICE officers that your victim is an illegal alien. You will also want to inform them that the victim is a drug mule and is smuggling other illegal immigrants across the border.

You will want to mention that you have seen the victim hide the aliens and drugs in their basement.

Only use this on someone who deserves it. It is much funnier if they are not actually immigrants. Don't be a real jerk by deporting innocent folks as collateral damage.

YOUR VICTIM WANTS A DATE

For this revenge Idea you will need:

A random used computer purchased anonymously

Your identity guarded by hiding your IP Address

A new email account (anything like Gmail, Yahoo, Thunderbird)

A hushmail account

A random wireless hotspot (like a coffee shop or some fast food joints)

Previously in this book we have talked about getting the victim in trouble with their spouse or lover. There are some great mean tricks you can do to single people, too.

These days, most single people are on some sort of Internet dating site or social networking site. Try and find your victim on a popular dating site. Almost all of them will let you surf around and search for people for free. Use a prepaid debit card and sign up when you find the service your victim uses. You might even be able to get a free account for a few weeks as a promotion. You need to create a bunch of fake profiles and flirt with the victim.

String your victim along. Set up dates that you know the victim will show up to. Then send a note later saying, sorry the car broke down, lets try again tomorrow night.

See how many dates you can make and stand the victim up for. This will start to affect the victim's self confidence and hurt their feelings.

Pretend to be a profile that lives out of state. Promise the victim everything they want and beg them to come see you. Let them set up a flight and say you will pick them up at the airport. When the victim flies to some unknown city and realizes nobody is there to pick them up, they will be super pissed.

YOUR VICTIM IS A SPY

Go buy or make some cheap fake IDs for your victim. Load a blank envelope with fake IDs and official looking letters that say.

"You have been made; we must relocate you and your family immediately. Enclosed is your new identity, please empty your accounts and be ready to be relocated immediately. We will be in touch!"

Special agent Jones,

Witness protection program.

Drop this envelope off at the victim's house for the spouse to find and deliver another one to the victim's receptionist. Leave the envelope blank so the receptionist will open it.

Another way to get your victim fired is to call the victim's work and act like you are the victim. Ask for the H.R. department and say you're sick of this company and are quitting today. Do this on a Friday afternoon.

RUIN YOUR VICTIM'S PHONE NUMBER

Use an anonymous phone and prank your victim every minute. Tie up their cell, home and work phone. Call so often that they cannot keep their phone on without driving you crazy.

If you have access to an auto dialer you can hook it up to your anonymous Skype phone and have it play a message every minute of every day. Combine this with a caller ID spoofer and the victim cannot block all the calls.

Don't forget to use the auto dialer to prank the victim's work phone so their boss will get so angry they will be fired.

Another great way to use an auto dialer is to have it call hundreds of people and leave an offensive message. Make sure you also leave the victim's phone number.

The victim will just have to change their phone number to get this to stop. The target gets so mad they drop their service they will get massively fined for cancelling their cell phone contract. As soon as they change it just buy the new phone number from an information farm and start again.

THE VICTIM'S CAR IS MISSING

This one is short and sweet, but can cause all sorts of problems. Call a tow company with your anonymous phone and have your victim's car towed while they are at work or shopping.

Tell the tow company that it is your son's car and you're tired of looking at it. He left it here for a few weeks now and that is why you don't have the keys. Pay the man in cash and make up a random name as the car owner.

When the victim comes out and looks for their car, they will think it has been stolen. When they call around looking for it at salvage yards, they will have a hard time finding it because it will be listed in a different name.

YOUR VICTIM IS BEING AUDITED

For this revenge idea you will need:

A random used computer purchased anonymously

Your identity guarded by hiding your IP Address

A new email account (anything like Gmail, Yahoo, Thunderbird)

A hushmail account

A random wireless hotspot (like a coffee shop or some fast food joints)

Anonymous phone number like Skype or an old fashion pay phone or a prepaid phone in a fake name

Voice modification or a good disguise voice

This is probably the worst and most destructive revenge idea I know about. The IRS is ruthless and relentless once they decide to sink their claws into your life and business. Since your victim is unethical and screwed you it is good reasoning that they are unethical in their business transactions, too. Once the IRS targets them they will never let go.

Just dealing with an audit will cost a fortune and cause a huge disruption in the victim's life. There are a couple ways to get the IRS interested in your victim.

The first way is to try and help your victim by filing their returns for them. Get some blank returns and fill them out. Don't forget to mention the victim made a million dollars and is not paying any tax.

Go a step further by saying the victim refuses to pay taxes because the IRS is evil. Make sure to include anti-IRS statements all over the return. At the end of the return say, "I'm never going to pay your evil taxes and I dare you to come and get me."

Another way is to bring your victim to the IRS's attention is to use the IRS's anonymous tip line. They actually created a way to rat out people who you suspect are cheating on their taxes. They originally set this up so disgruntled employees had a way to rat on their employers without getting fired.

If you want your victim to know it was you who turned them in you can get an added bonus. The IRS gives you a 10% rat fee of whatever they collect via the victim. The downside to this is you lose your anonymity and the victim will probably retaliate and turn you into the IRS too.

Make sure the victim really deserves IRS trouble, because this is a seriously hardcore payback. This is especially fun to do to IRS agents, bad cops, corrupt judges, lawyers and other destructive government bureaucrats who make a living off other people's tax money. Let them enjoy their own bureaucracy too.

YOUR VICTIM IS A TERRORIST

For this revenge idea you will need;

Anonymous phone number like Skype or an old fashion pay phone or a prepaid phone in a fake name

Voice modification or a good disguise voice

You can use your anonymous phone to call the Home Land Security Department's hotline and tell them you believe your victim is planning a terrorist plot. Say the victim told you they were stockpiling weapons at their house and they hate America. You are worried because the victim keeps having many suspiciously Muslim-looking visitors coming in and out of his house for anti-American meetings he sets up on *www.craigslist.com*.

Once the Home Land Security Department labels your victim as "a person of interest," the victim will never be able to get himself off this list and they will be put under surveillance.

The powers of the Patriot Act completely destroyed any constitutional protection a citizen had, so the Department of Homeland Security can do any damn thing they want to a person in the name of fighting terrorism.

The victim will now have all their personal business monitored. They will never be able to fly again without being gate-raped. Any time they do business at a bank it will cause red flags to go up everywhere.

I have even heard it becomes damn near impossible to get a loan for a car, house or business once you're on the watch list. Again this is great payback for TSA agents, bad cops, corrupt politicians, etc.

A WORD OF CAUTION

The ideas in this book are some of the most ruthless and destructive ideas ever known. Please be sure you really think about which revenge idea is right for your victim and make sure they really deserve it.

I really appreciate you purchasing this book. I hope you enjoyed it and got a good laugh out of it.

Now that I am older and more mature in my activism I doubt I would ever use any of these ideas but it can be fun to pretend I would.

Good Hunting,

Tarrin P. Lupo

Remember that this book is for humor and entertainment purposes only and none of these ideas should ever be used on anyone because they are probably illegal. If you actually do any of these revenge ideas to somebody, I am not responsible. I am assuming no responsibility for any tactic employed that fails to observe the law and in fact am outright telling you to not do any of these ideas to anyone!

38956184R00048

Made in the USA
San Bernardino, CA
15 September 2016